Funny Mom

QUOTES COLORING BOOK

Belongs to :

_____

OUR GIFT FOR YOU

EMAIL US AT:
KIDSMARTER.INTERNATIONAL@GMAIL.COM
TO RECEIVE FREE OF CHARGE A COLORING E-BOOK
TITLE THE EMAIL: MOM COLORING BOOK
AND WE'LL SEND SOME GOODIES YOUR WAY!

Thank you!
I hope you enjoy our book and spend wonderful moments coloring it!
Your feedback is very important to us, please let us know how you like our book.

never
BORED
always
TIRED

I got it all together

but I forgot where I put it

#momlife

I live in a
MADHOUSE
run by a
tiny Army
i made myself
MOM LIFE

This Mom RUNS ON Coffee And Wine

every great
MOM
drops the
F·BOMB

Hold on !
LET ME
OVERTHINK
this

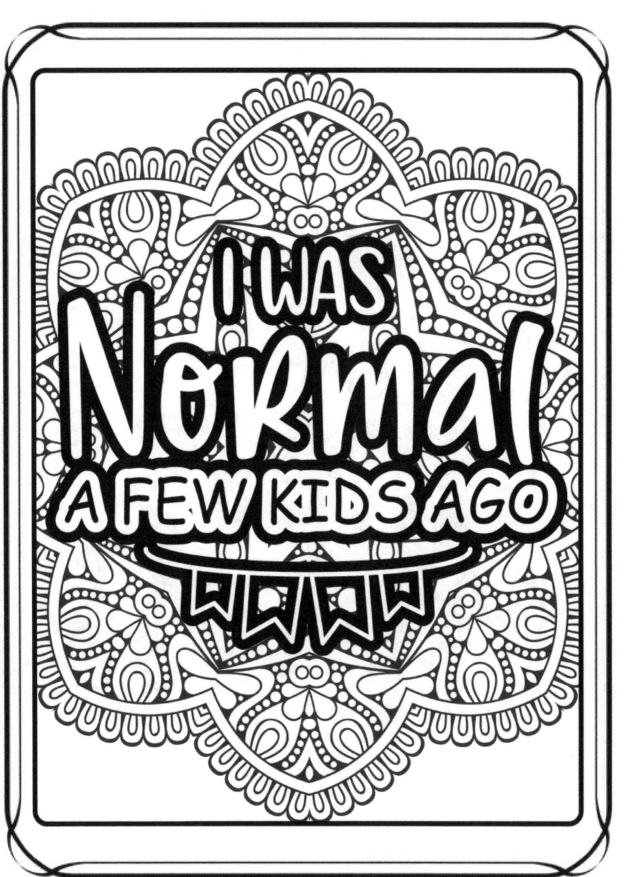

hot mess express

TO THE **WORLD**
YOU ARE A
Mother
BUT TO YOUR **FAMILY**
YOU ARE THE
World

I'M NOT LIKE A REGULAR MOM I'M A COOL MOM

KINDA classy KINDA HOOD

LASHES
longer
than my
PATIENCE

TERRIBLE TWOS

mama OF DRAMA #girlmom

Messy bun AND getting STUFF DONE

MOM HARD
wife hard
WORK HARD
everyday

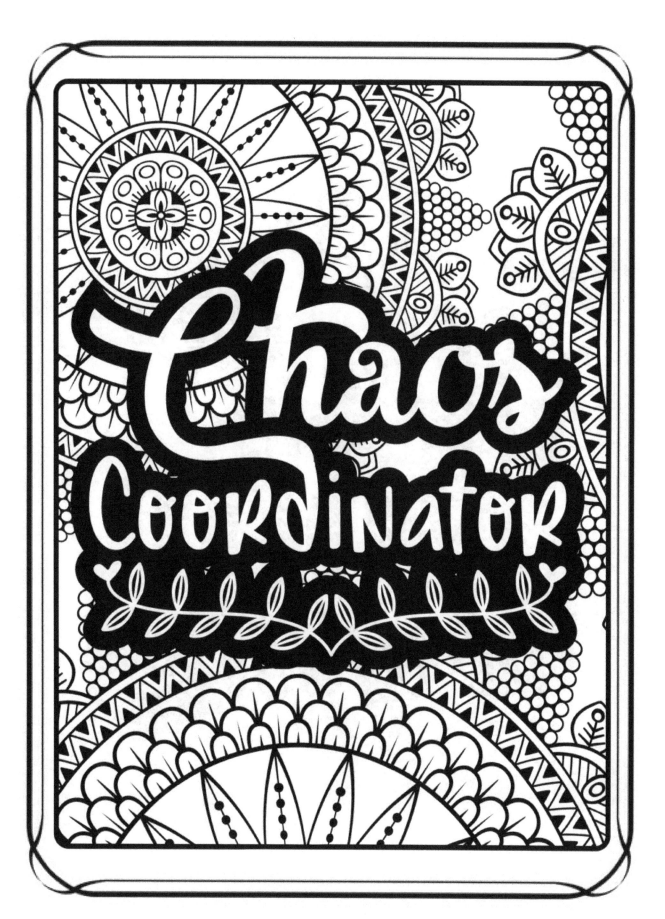

JUST A
Good Mom
with a
HOOD
playlist

"HIDING IN THE BATHROOM WITH THE DOOR LOCKED, EATING NUTELLA. NOT EVEN EMBARRASSED."

I may be
WRONG
BUT
I Doubt It

SILENCE IS GOLDEN.

UNLESS YOU HAVE KIDS.

THAN SILENCE IS SUSPICIOUS.

AMAZING LOVING STRONG HAPPY SELFLESS GRACEFUL

YOU NEVER REALIZE HOW WEIRD YOU ARE UNTIL YOU HAVE A KID, WHO ACTS JUST LIKE YOU

I gotta ♡
good heart
but this
mouth

"I'M A REALLY GREAT MOM UNTIL MY KIDS GET UP IN THE MORNING."

Love my Tribe

"A MOTHER'S LOVE IS UNCONDITIONAL,
HER TEMPER IS ANOTHER SUBJECT"

mom
BOSS
CEO

'SOME DAYS YOU'LL BE A ROCK STAR EMPLOYEE. SOME DAYS YOU'LL BE A ROCK STAR MAMA. AND SOME DAYS YOU'LL BE A ROCK STAR AT BOTH.'

Slay
AT
HOME
Mom

'I USED TO BE COOL . NOW,
I'M A TINY PERSON'S SNACK BICH'

Oh Honey,
I am
That
mom

I WONDER HOW OFTEN MY
KIDS LOOK AT ME AND
THINK
"THIS BITCH IS CRAZY"

JUST another manic Mom Day

WHEN A KID SAYS
"DADDY, I WANT MOMMY"
THAT'S THE KID VERSION OF
"I'D LIKE TO SPEAK TO YOUR SUPERVISOR"

Nap time
IS MY
happy
HOUR
zᶻᶻ

MOTHER
hustler

BRA OFF
HAIR UP
SWEATS ON
POP CORK

UNICORNS
and
BULLS
#momofboth

GIRLS:

ALL DRAMA, HARD TO KEEP MOM ALIVE."

"BOYS: LESS DRAMA THAN GIRLS, HARD TO KEEP ALIVE.

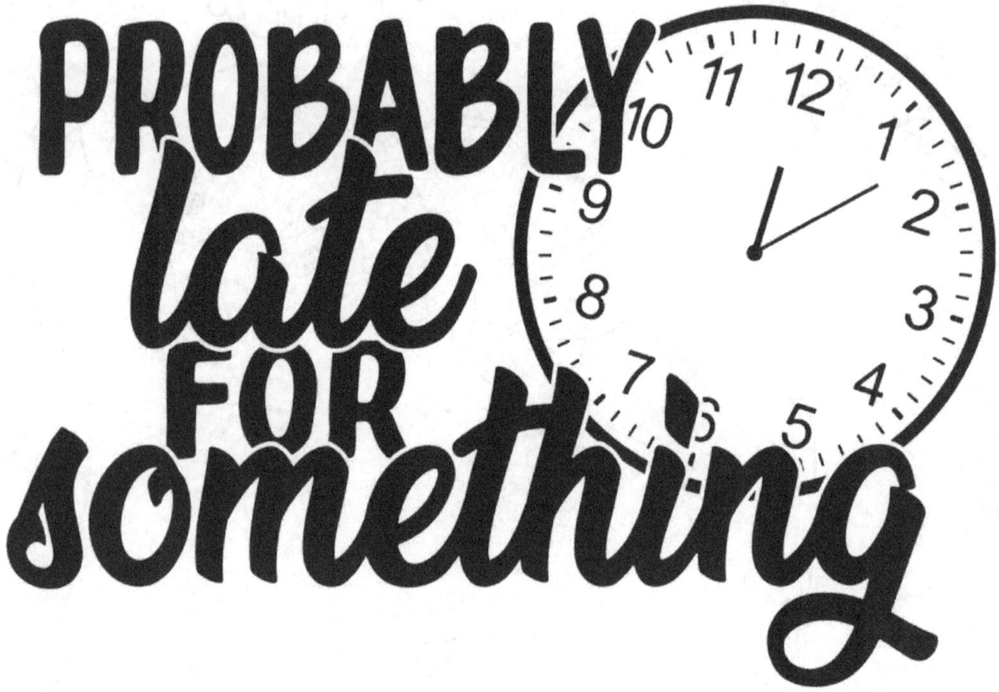
PROBABLY
late
FOR
something

"DON'T YELL AT YOUR KIDS. LEAN IN AND WHISPER. IT IS MUCH SCARIER."

Beauty
& Beast
#momofboth

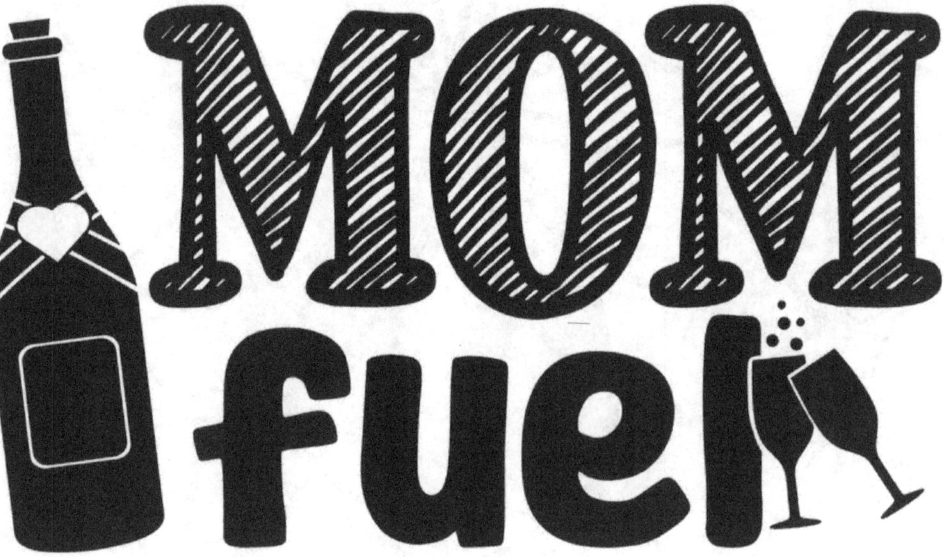
MOM
fuel

mommin'
AIN'T EASY ♡

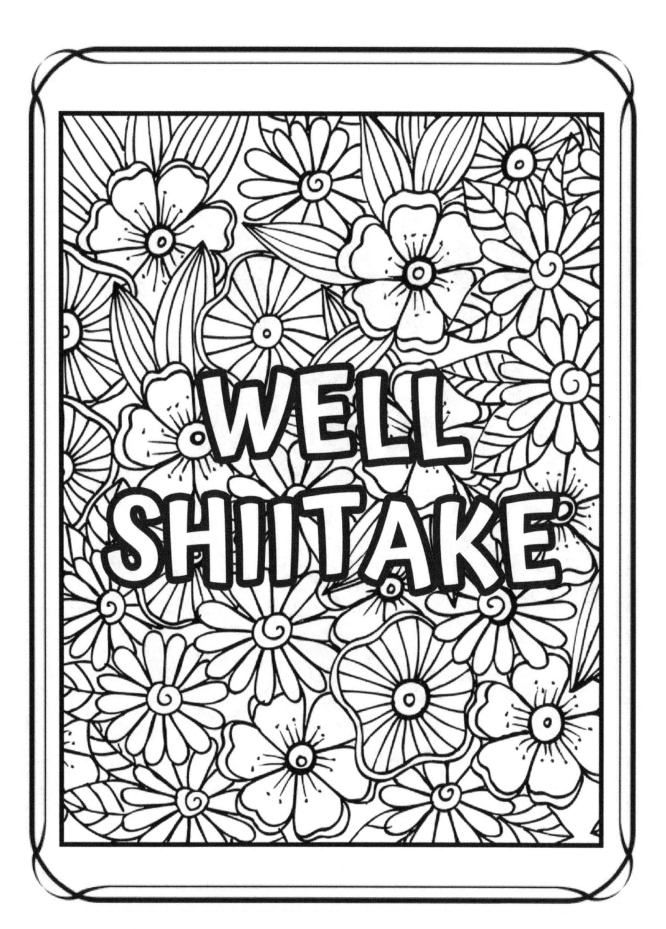

mom
of
boys

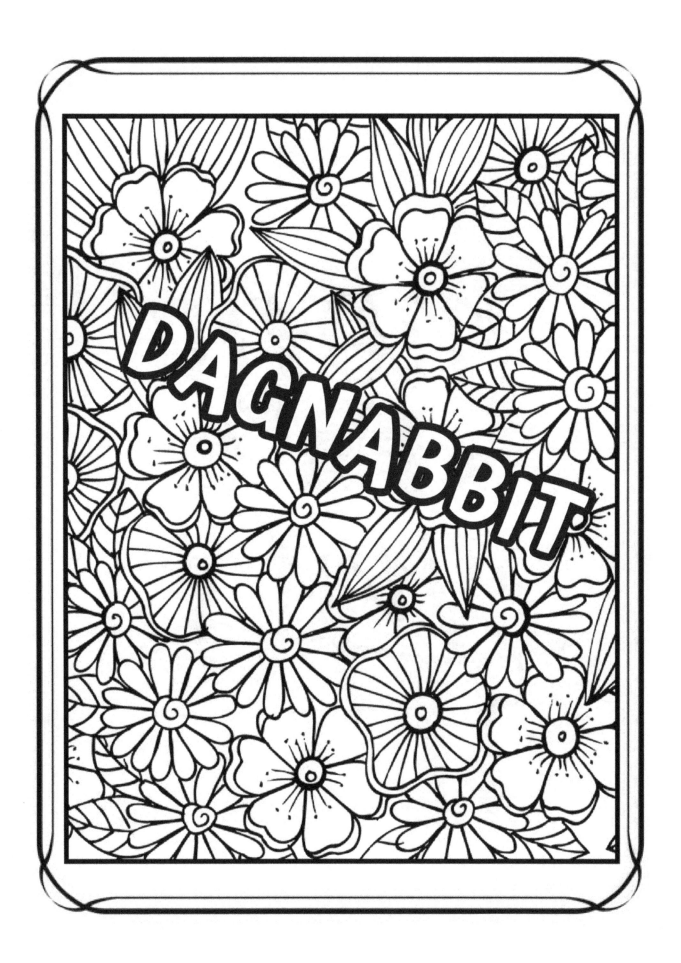

mom
of
girls

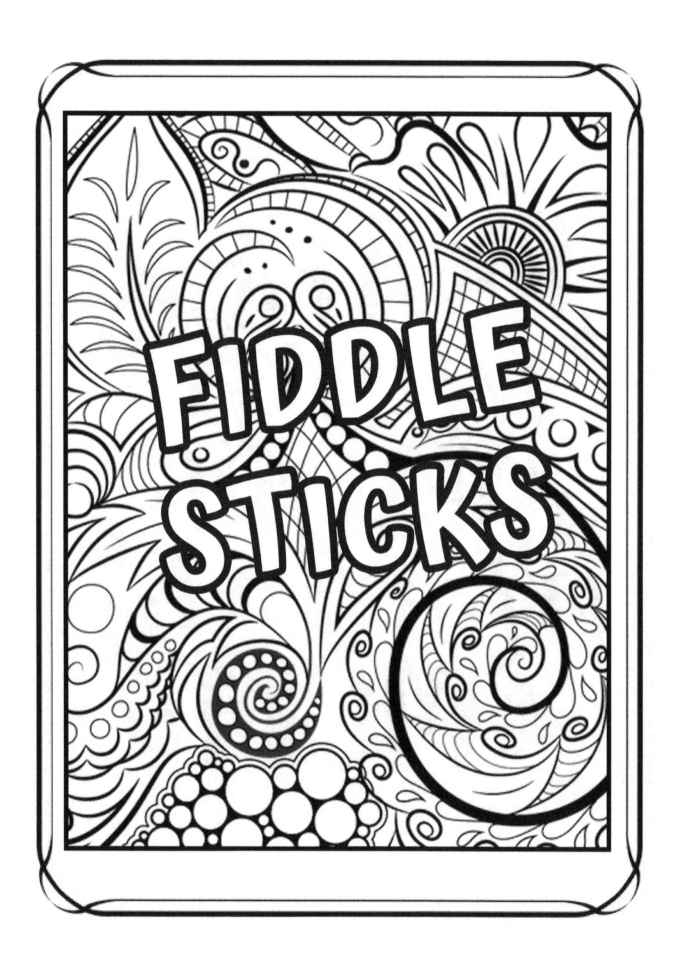

MOTHER
Mama
MADRE
Mommy
MOM

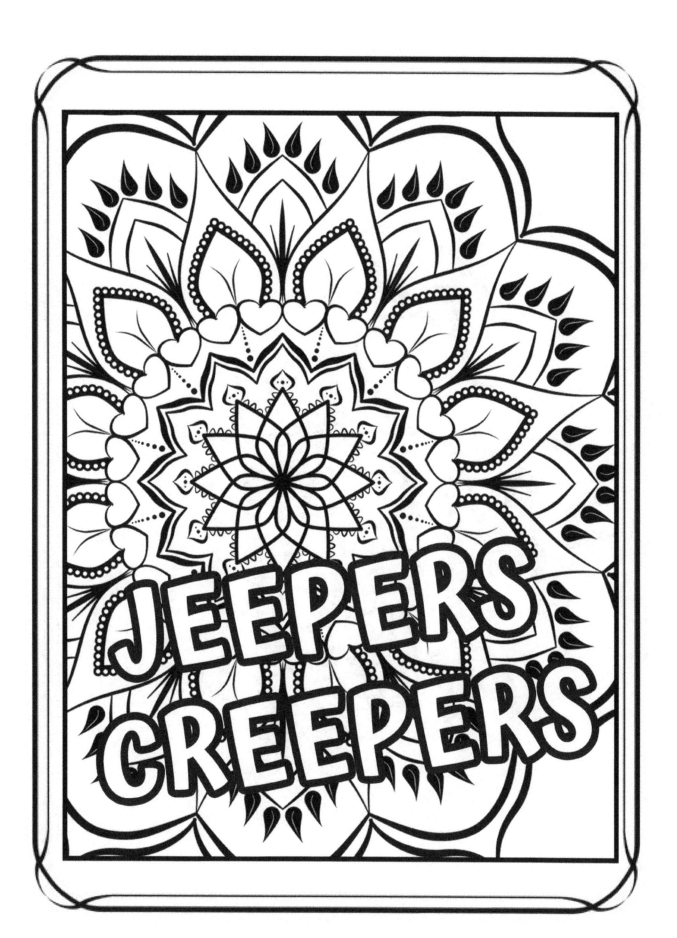

I WAS NORMAL 1 Kid AGO

CRUD

MY GREATEST
blessings
CALL ME
Mom

FIRST
my mother
FOREVER
my friend

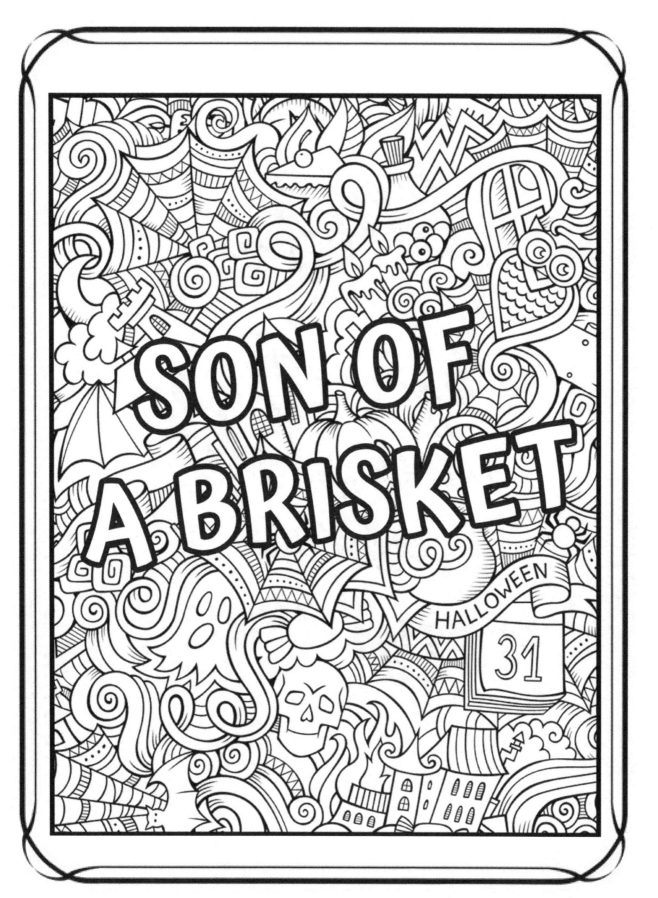

OMG...

my mother
was right
about
everything...

Blessed Mama

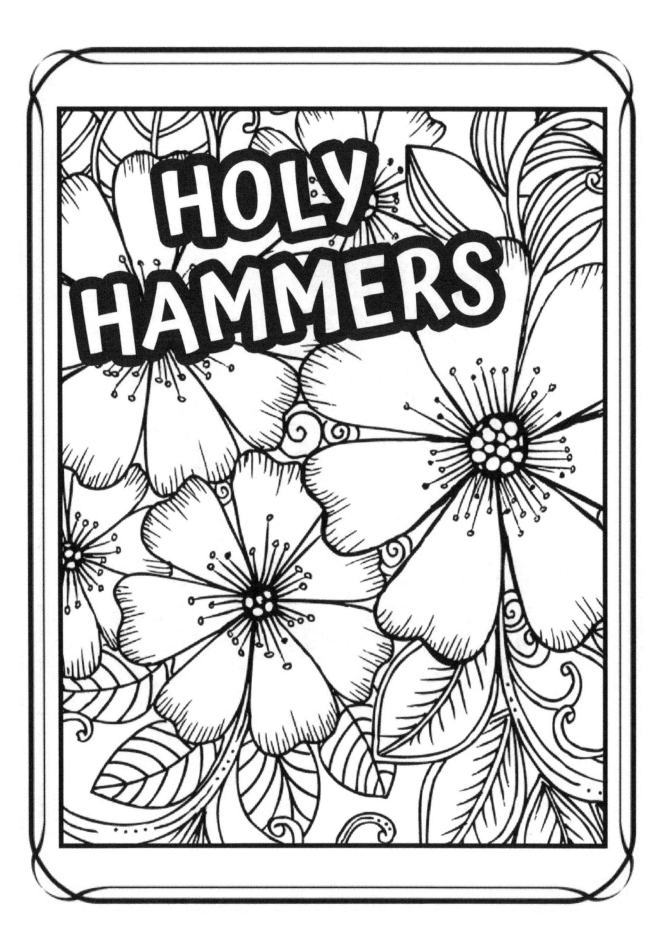

WIFE
mother
COFFEE
lover

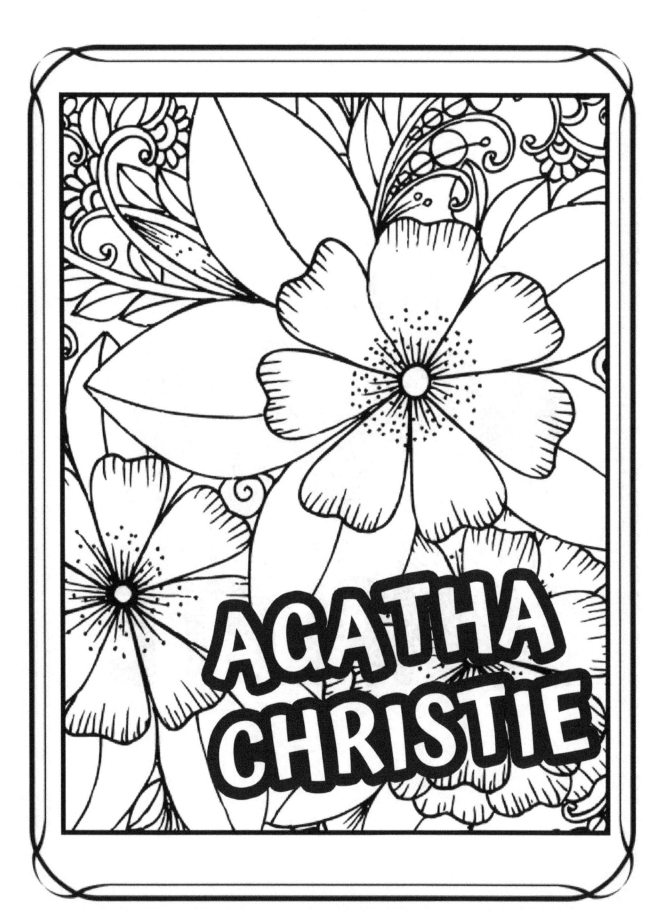

Being a M♥M makes my life COMPLETE

DOMESTIC *gangsta* ♥

DOG MOTHER wine lover